F. E. O. L.

"FOUR ELEMENTS OF LIFE"

Vol. 1

The Creation Of New Superheroes

Created & Written by
Teddy G. Mazloum

"EarthMan"

"OceanMan"

"FireGirl"

"WindMan"

Chapter One

It all started when the black goldish stone from outer space entered our atmosphere straight into the desert.

The government took control of the stone without anyone noticing under the supervision of General Madix; who's handling the department of science and technology.

The General divided the stone into four sections and wanted to test them on living human beings by force; which made his personal assistant Bob, to act fast on helping and rescuing them.

Bob set the lab on fire, freed the prisoners, and escaped with the stones which were boiled and turned into liquids.

While Bob was running away from the wounded general; he decided to hide the liquids under a certain tree next to a foster house and marked them so he can find them again.

Next day four kids from the foster house were playing next to the tree. One of them was always bullied because he had a scar on his eye and a bit of weak muscles.

He got attacked by a bigger and stronger kid; and was pushed hard toward the tree. Accidently, he found the liquids and they were all bedazzled.

Each one of the kids drank a different color which gave them unimaginable superpowers.

The scar eyed kid Jake drank the green liquid and became Windman. He could control the wind in life.

The bully Tom drank the orange liquid and became Earthman. He could control the sand, trees and mostly everything on the ground.

The other kid Tyron drank the blue liquid and became Oceanman. He could control the sea or any water existed.

Last but not least, the beautiful little girl Jenny, who is secretly in love with Windman, drank the red liquid and became Firegirl. She can control fire and create it also.

The world was introduced to new superheroes and were pleased by them as they grew up strong on fighting crime and defending the innocent alongside the government

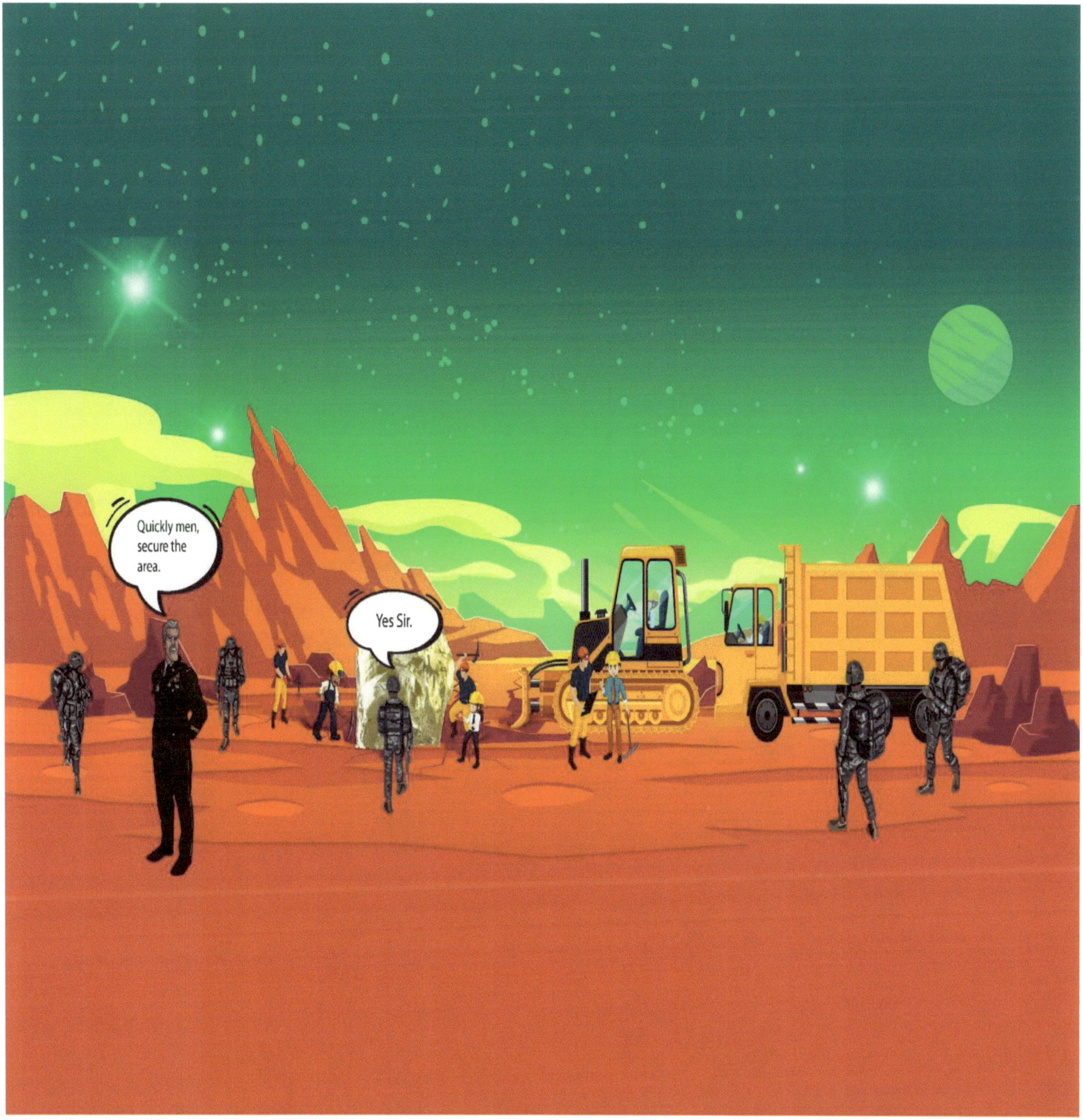
Quickly men, secure the area.
Yes Sir.

Finally my greatest discovery ...HAHA
Indeed General, indeed..but what to do with this extraordinary stone?

I MUST TAKE THESE LIQUIDS OF THE STONE AND HIDE THEM FROM HIM.
FOSTER HOUSE

Chapter Two

As years passed on, General Madix was always secretly creating sea & underground monsters and robots; advanced equipped villains, to fight the F.E.O.L and trying to destroy them. His secret plan was to take out the liquids from their bodies and take them to himself.

Windman was always the moody guy and used to get into a lot of fights with the others except for Firegirl. He liked her also but never admitted.

One time while they were fighting a highly advanced sea monster robot, Windman was very angry and decided to kill the human inside the robot. Directly the others tried stopping him and got him even madder since he knows he's not a match against all three together.

He left and was walking alone on the beach where he met an old sick guy. This latter approached Windman and started filling his head with poisonous ideas that he should possess all the liquids to himself in order to defeat the others.

Windman was poisoned and convinced by the old man; in which he didn't know that he was disguised and indeed secretly General Madix; who finally got his chance for revenge.

Windman decided to fight them one by one and bring them back to the General's lab; where the latter promised to give him all the powers.

Windman fought Oceonman and Earthman one by one very hard battles, and was able to defeat them. Firegirl fought him also and could have defeated him, but her broken-heart prevented her to proceed and surrendered to him.

Now as they are all in the lab sleeping separately next to each others with the right equipment attached to them, General Madix tricked Windman and took all the liquids from the four of them straight into his body.

Now General Madix became EVIL FEOL and can control all four forces of nature. He left them weak and strangled and went to rule the world.

DAM THEM! They have my powers and I will not rest until I get them back.
Where are you hiding you weak fools! I will destroy all four of you.

Explore my wrath of fire you monster. BOOMMM
Time to say goodbye to Earth, I'll throw you away to outer space where you will be vanished. VOOM VOOOMMM
Arise my quick sands and capture this Monster's legs.
vortex. I'll control his arms also, get him .

Why? My lovely Dolphins. I will get you for this. My great sharks; Attackkkk !!
Prepare for your destruction Seaboy.
In that case, Arrise my massive tornadoes. All together combine and swipe this tiny whirlpool.
I will crush them easily!
Noo! That's it, it's time for my rage of whirlpools. Arrise!
Why are you doing this? We are a great team.
You are all weak. I don't need you or this team. Now vanishh !

What are you going to do with them?
Great job my son, I always knew you are the best.
I like the sound of that.
Don't worry. I'll just remove the liquid from their bodies and transfer them to you; and you'll be the strongest ever.
Good! Now quickly put them in the machines and you sit in the last one for the beginning of the tranformation.

HAHA! I am Genral Madix now and I'm the strongest person ever. I can feel the power inside me and now I can control all four elements of life together.

Chapter Three

While they were all blaming Windman for what he did and he was ashamed and full of regret, out of nowhere BOB appeared after all these years.

BOB had split the liquids when he hid them and took the other half with him just in case of any emergency; which in this case is.

So he gave them back his powers but they refused to let Windman join them with their quest against the crazy general. They couldn't trust him anymore.

The 3 of them were no match for the great EVIL FEOL. Every time one of them uses their power, he would reverse it against them. Finally when they were losing and about to be destroyed....

Out of nowhere Windman appears to the rescue; striking the general with everything of power he possess. He gave them hope and unity.

Now all four of them are fighting together side by side destroying the general.

Earth man controlled EVIL FEOL's hands through the sand and rocks, Oceonman controlled his legs through the water from the sea, and Windman was controlling his body through the wind and using it as ropes.

There was still Firegirl to strike her final blow; which is more heater than the volcano's lava. She's hesitating because if she does; Windman will be also destroyed with the general since he's very close and attached to him.

Until she heard Windman saying that he loved her and will always be with her, but she has to strike her shot to save the world. So she sadly did.

General Madix was destroyed and his body returned into normal shape. Windman disappeared and nowhere to be found. Everyone sadly knew that he was gone.

Time passed on... up high in the mountains, an old man with his wife were driving in their truck under heavy snowy storm.

An avalanche happened nearby and a huge rock was dropping on them, when suddenly it moved by its own away from them.

They stopped in the middle of the road in shock when they saw a green-suited man flying near them into the sky.

He lives. Windman lives.....

On the other hand, far away from Earth on a creepy distant planet, a huge ferocious sound was screaming: "WHERE IS MY PRECIOUS STONE"......

To be continued...

I suggest we join the army and try to help them.
Are you crazy? We're no heroes anymore. One blow from the General and we will die.
At least we would have tried. There's no shame in it...
Stop it you guys, we should think of a better plan...

What do you mean?
Hey, what are you doing here?
I was the general's old partner and I had to betray him; that crazy power seeker.
Don't worry my childern... I'm not here to harm you but instead to help.
I can sense that you know a way to stop the general.

I know what I did is wrong I'm sorry you guys. Please give me another chance.
No way, we'll not trust that traitor again.
What? So you still have the second half now?
No way!
Well I was the one who hid the liquid from him, but it was only half the amount.
I forgive you Jake, I know you more than the others. You all know that we can't win without him.
It's time you have your powers back, but believe me; It will take all four of you to beat the general.

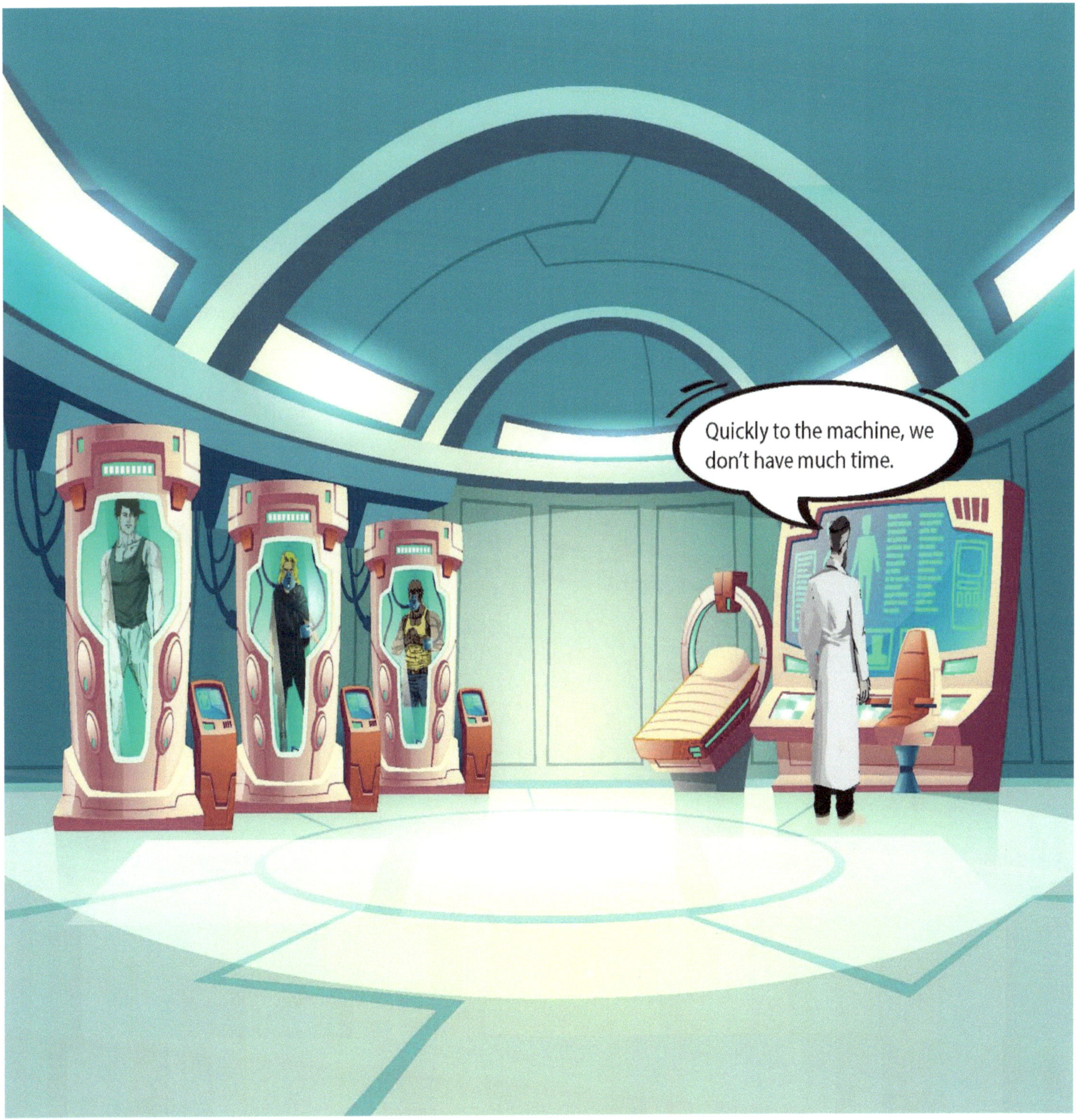
Quickly to the machine, we don't have much time.

I see you got help from that snake partner of mine and had your powers again. It doesn't matter; I'll enjoy destroying you all.

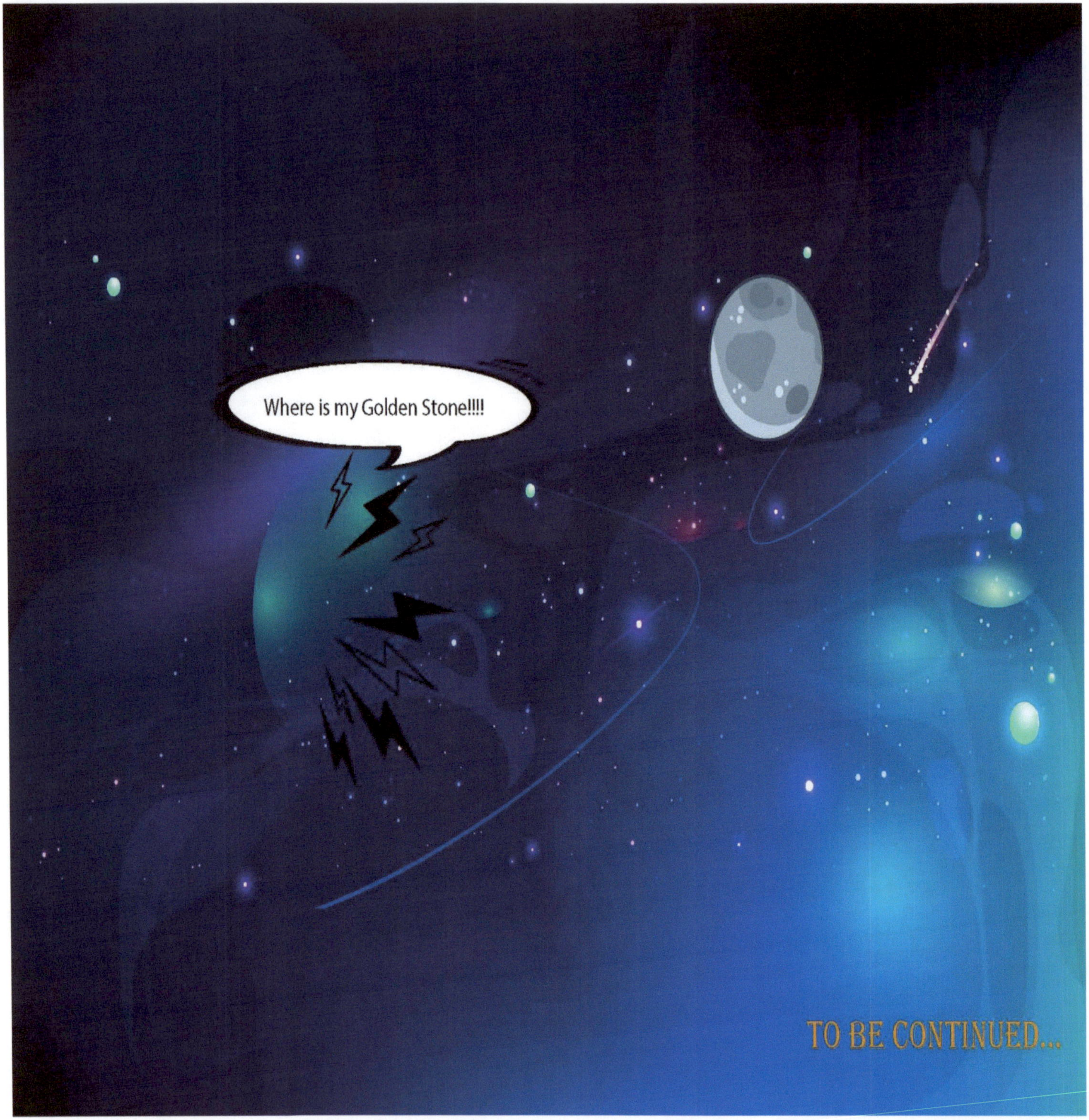
Where is my Golden Stone!!!!
TO BE CONTINUED...

This newly marvelous journey was simply a combination of fantasy and ideas from my humble imagination; to turn it into an enjoyable and pleasurable reality.

A Special **Thanks** and **Gratitude** for everyone who is sharing Interest in my new story and concept, and I will always appreciate your support.

Always believe in yourself and remember there's a unique superhero hidden in each and every one of us, stay positive, and May the ultimate power in our universe be always with you.

See you soon in Vol **2 Rise of the Dark Reaper**
Teddy G. Mazloum

www.ingramcontent.com/pod-product-compliance
Lightning Source LLC
Chambersburg PA
CBHW042012080426
42734CB00002B/52